D1367229

Animals of the Night

VAMPIRE BATS AFTER DARK

Heather M. Moore Niver

Enslow Publishing
101 W. 23rd Street
Suite 240
New York, NY 10011
USA

enslow.com

Words to Know

calcar—A bony part of a bat's heel that it uses to hold on when it is upside down. It also helps a bat fly by holding up its tail so it doesn't drag in the wind.

carnivorous—Meat-eating.

colony—A group of one kind of animal living together.

habitat— The place in which an animal lives.

mammal—An animal that has a backbone and hair, usually gives birth to live babies, and produces milk to feed its young.

New World—Relating to North and South America.

nocturnal—Mostly active at night.

prey—An animal hunted by another animal for food.

regurgitate—To bring up food a second time after it has been swallowed.

roost—To settle in to sleep for the night, sometimes in a group.

species—A particular kind of animal.

tropical—Relating to very hot and humid areas.

Contents

Midnight Feast

The moon rises and lights up the dark night. From within a hollow tree, the vampire bats wake up. It's time to dine. Swooping out into the night, the common vampire bat uses special senses on its face and nose to find warm-blooded animals. It lands on the ground near its next meal. Its strong legs help it crawl on the back of a sleeping animal. Its teeth are so sharp the animal doesn't feel a thing. Dinner is served. The bat laps up the blood until it is full. When it's done eating, it flies off into the night.

Vampire bats emerge at night to hunt for their next meal of blood.

Behold, the Vampire Bat

Vampire bats are pretty special. It is the only **mammal** that makes its dinner on blood alone. The vampire bat is one of only three kinds of **carnivorous** bats. There are three kinds of vampire bats: common vampire bat, the hairy-legged vampire bat, and the white-winged vampire bat. These are the only bats that drink blood.

Vampire bats are very small. In fact, their bodies are usually smaller than a human's thumb. They often have dark brown or black fur on their bodies. The fur on their bellies is usually a lighter color.

FUN FACT!

Bats are the only mammals that can fly.

Vampire bats lick up blood as it flows out of an animal. They don't need to suck it out.

The wings of a vampire bat are long compared to its body. Its body is only 3.5 inches (9 centimeters) long. Its wings spread 7 inches (18 cm). The vampire bat's wings have bones like fingers. They are covered with a thin skin. They also have one claw that works like a thumb. It sticks out the front of the wing. The bat can use it to move around.

The legs of the vampire bat are special. They are long and strong. Their back legs also help them take off and fly.

FUN FACT!

The biggest **New World** bat is called the American false vampire bat. Its wings are more than 24 inches (60 cm) across!

Long wings help the vampire bat swoop through the night.

Vampire bats have very small ears and a tiny tail. They have a short nose that is shaped like a cone. Every part of a vampire bat is small. They weigh less than 2 ounces (about 57 grams).

Vampire bats in movies look very scary, but most of their features are not like real ones. Vampire bats do have a wide mouth. When they open it, you can see their teeth. This might look scary. The vampire bat has very sharp front teeth. Their back teeth are short and not very sharp.

FUN FACT!

When a vampire bat eats, its weight can double!

Vampire bats have almost twenty teeth. They have the least teeth of any other bat.

Where in the World Is the Vampire Bat?

Vampire bats live all over the continent of South America. They live in **tropical** areas, but they can live in dry or steamy **habitats**, too.

Like most bats, vampire bats are **nocturnal**. They spend their days in hollow trees, caves, mines, and sometimes in old buildings. A group of bats living together is called a **colony**. Sometimes more than one **species**, or kind, of bat lives in the same place. Usually different kinds of bats keep to themselves, though. This helps keep peace among bats.

FUN FACT!

A colony of bats can include as many as 1,000 bats!

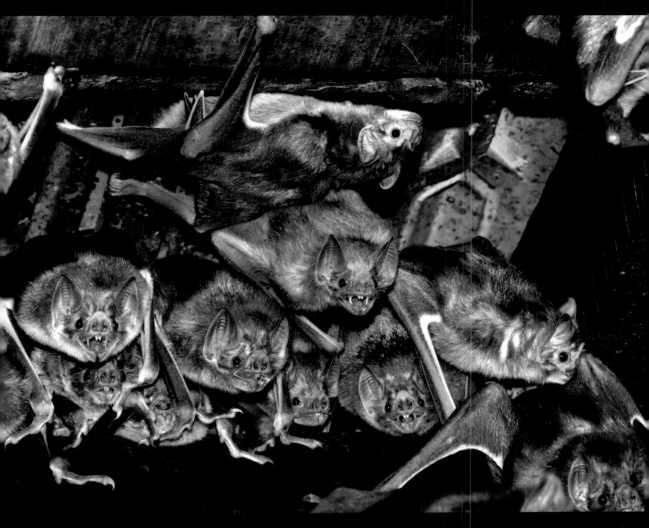

Groups of vampires bats live, or nest, together in sheltered areas.

On the Hunt

After a vampire bat is done **roosting** all day, it's time to hunt! They use the moon's light to find their **prey**. They are very strong fliers. Their arms and legs are shaped to help them move around easily and quickly on the ground, too.

Vampire bats fly about 3 feet (1 meter) above the ground looking for lunch. They are looking for another mammal. When they find one, they land on the ground nearby. Their noses are good at sensing heat. This helps them bite where there is a vein full of blood.

A vampire bat's teeth are so sharp that its prey usually can't even feel the bite. This bat is feeding on a cow's leg.

A vampire bat bites when its prey is sleeping. Then the bat immediately jumps back, in case the animal wakes up! If its prey stays asleep, the vampire bat begins to lap up the blood. They do not suck the blood out. Their tongues have grooves that help them lick up the blood.

Special chemicals in the bat's saliva make the bite numb. The prey doesn't feel the bite and wake up. These chemicals also keep the blood from getting too thick. The vampire bat might feed for thirty minutes. When it's done eating, the vampire bat is almost too full to fly!

FUN FACT!

Scientists are studying how the chemical in a vampire bat's saliva can help human heart patients!

A vampire bat can drink about 1 teaspoon (25 milliliters) of blood in half an hour.

Echo! Echo! Echo!

Vampire bats have another handy trick for flying around in the dark night. This is known as echolocation. They use very high-pitched sounds. Vampire bats make these sounds when they are flying. Then they listen for how the sounds bounce off solid objects. As the sounds bounce back, they can tell where objects are. This way, they don't fly into them. These sounds are so high that humans cannot hear them. Echolocation helps them find prey, too. Vampire bats also use smell and heat to locate mammals.

FUN FACT!

Other kinds of bats also use echolocation to fly around at night.

Vampire bats use sound in the night to tell where prey and other objects are located in the dark.

Where Do They Dine?

The common vampire bat is the only vampire bat that enjoys its meals on the ground. White-winged vampire bats enjoy their dinners in trees. They like to eat chicken blood. They wait for one to settle down to sleep in a tree. The white-winged bat creeps up from underneath by crawling on the bottom of the branch. As soon as it is underneath the bird, it bites. It bites the back part of the chicken's foot where a toe sticks out.

FUN FACT!

White-winged bats also sometimes snuggle in with a sleeping chicken. The sleepy hen thinks the bat is a baby and lets it near her belly. Then the bat bites.

White-winged vampire bats have a couple of handy tricks for enjoying a meal from a chicken. You can see the bat in this photo holding onto the branch while it sneaks a meal from the bird.

Hairy-legged vampire bats also like to dine in trees, but they are not as sneaky as their white-winged relatives. The hairy-legged bat lands right on the bird. They hang upside down and drink from the bottom of the bird. It is able to hang on thanks to a handy extra bony part of its heel. It is called a **calcar**. The calcar also helps it fly better. Some bats don't have a calcar. Other bats do, but they might be all different sizes.

Hairy-legged bats don't mind eating dinner upside down in the air.

Share and Share Alike

You will never have to remind a vampire bat to share. They do it naturally! Sometimes they share dinner with each other. A mother bat will **regurgitate** blood for her young until it is old enough to hunt on its own. Sometimes adult vampire bats do this for a bat in their group that did not get to eat. Vampire bats remember who shared and who did not. Sometimes one bat enjoys food from another but does not return the favor.

FUN FACT!

Vampire bats that do not share with the group may not be treated as well as the other bats that do share.

Vampire bats look out for others in their group. Sometimes they feed one another.

Baby Bats

A mother vampire bat usually has one baby at a time. In the wild they care for their babies for about five months. In zoos they do this for up to nine months. Vampire bats are like other mammals. The babies drink their mother's milk. When they are old enough, they start to drink blood. Vampire bat females are good mothers. They will care for another baby bat if its own mother is missing.

FUN FACT!

Baby vampire bats cling to their mothers for the first three months, even when mom is flying!

Vampire bats live for up to twelve years in the wild. In protected places like zoos, they may live for twenty years.

Hunted

Sometimes vampire bats have to look out to make sure they don't become prey. They can be hunted right in thin air by large birds such as hawks and eagles. Sometimes snakes find them in the caves where they sleep. Humans are their main threat, though. Because bats drink from their animals, such as cows, farmers try to poison the bats. The poisons, called vampiricides, spread through a whole colony of bats. Hundreds of bats can die.

FUN FACT!

Many bats around the world are dying from a disease called "white nose syndrome." So far, vampire bats are not at risk, but scientists are keeping a close watch on them.

If one bat is poisoned, it can spread the poison to many other bats in its colony.

Stay Safe Around Vampire Bats

It doesn't happen very often, but sometimes vampire bats do bite humans.

- Never handle a vampire bat. They will bite to defend themselves.
- If you see a bat on the ground, it may be sick. Never pick up a bat with bare hands.
- If a bat bites you, go to the doctor immediately!
- If you wake up with a bat in your room, it is smart to have an adult catch the bat. Have the bat tested for disease. Tell a doctor you have been exposed to a bat, even if you are not sure whether it bit you.

Learn More

Books

Lynette, Rachel. *Vampire Bats*. New York: Powerkids Press, 2013.

Niver, Heather Moore. *We Need Bats*. New York: PowerKids Press, 2016.

Rake, Jodi S. *Why Vampire Bats Suck Blood and Other Gross Facts About Animals*. Mankato, MN: Capstone Press, 2012.

Shea, Therese. *Bloodsucking Vampire Bats*. New York: Gareth Stevens, 2016.

Websites

Bat World

batworld.org/
Learn all about vampire bats and other interesting bats with photos and facts.

DKfindout! Vampire Bat

dkfindout.com/us/animals-and-nature/bats/vampire-bat/
Take a look at photos, facts, and interactive diagrams about vampire bats.

Cincinnati Zoo: Vampire Bat

cincinnatizoo.org/blog/animals/vampire-bat/
Check out facts, photos, and videos to learn more about vampire bats.

Index

Published in 2017 by Enslow Publishing, LLC.
101 W. 23rd Street, Suite 240, New York, NY 10011

Copyright © 2017 by Enslow Publishing, LLC.
All rights reserved.

No part of this book may be reproduced by any means without the
written permission of the publisher.

Library of Congress Cataloging-in-Publication Data
Names: Niver, Heather M. Moore.
Title: Vampire bats after dark / Heather M. Moore Niver.
Description: New York, NY : Enslow Publishing, 2017. | Series:
Animals of the night | Includes bibliographical references and index.
Identifiers: LCCN 2015051241| ISBN 9780766077119 (library
bound) | ISBN 9780766077416 (pbk.) | ISBN 9780766076877 (6-pack)
Subjects: LCSH: Vampire bats—Behavior—Juvenile literature. |
Vampire bats—Juvenile literature.
Classification: LCC QL737.C52 N58 2016 | DDC 599.4/5—dc23
LC record available at http://lccn.loc.gov/2015051241

Printed in the United States of America

To Our Readers: We have done our best to make sure all website
addresses in this book were active and appropriate when we went to
press. However, the author and the publisher have no control over and
assume no liability for the material available on those websites or on any
websites they may link to. Any comments or suggestions can be sent by
e-mail to customerservice@enslow.com.

Photo Credits: Throughout book, narvikk/E+/Getty Images (starry
background), kimberrywood/Digital Vision Vectors/Getty Images
(green moon dingbat); cover, pp. 1, 11 Minden Pictures/Minden
Pictures/SuperStock.com, samxmed/E+/Getty Images (moon); pp. 3,
7 Bruce Dale/National Geographic/Getty Images; p. 5 © Rick & Nora
Bowers/Alamy; pp. 9, 27 Günter Peters/ullstein bild/Getty Images; p.
13 Tony Camacho/Science Source; pp. 15, 17 © Ardea/Gordon, Nick/
Animals Animals; p. 19 Barry Mansell/Barry Mansell/SuperStock.com;
p. 21 Rexford Lord/Science Source; p. 23 James H. Robinson/Science
Source; p. 25 B. G. Thomson/Science Source; p. 29 Michael Lynch/
Shutterstock.com.